GOD TO THE HEART OF A HUSBAND

ISBN – 978-1-7336 203-2-1

Dedication

To my husband, my love, you have challenged me to go deeper, love deeper and live deeper. You are a gift from God I will forever value and treasure. To my dad, Ken Dewese you are a model example of God's love. You represent His heart well and your life draws others to the Father! In remembrance of Fernando Ramirez who now resides in heaven.

Preface

Things are continually changing as the immoral and loose standards of society swirl around us. It is important to remember who we serve and whose we are.

This book is all about God's heart and what He is saying to you as a husband. God loves you and your willingness to stand up and lead with righteousness brings great joy to His heart. As you read through this journal, try to visualize the heart of God speaking directly to you. It does not matter who you are, where you have been or what you have done. God sees you through the blood and He calls you a mighty man of valor, the head and not the tail.

I pray this book refreshes you as you spend time with God in His presence, embracing what the heart of God is saying to you as a husband. God is calling men to lead their families with strength and honor. He has placed a high value on you as a husband and your role is priceless to God. His heart is for your marriage and loving Him while leading with His heart is gold. Heaven is watching and cheering you on!

the prayer

OF A RIGHTEOUS PERSON

is powerful and effective.

JAMES 5:16

let all that
YOU DO BE
done in love
IICOR 16:18

you are

A MAN OF VALOR

Father God,

I ask you to help me love my wife today through your heart. As you gently lay things on my heart, I will love her with your goodness. Give me understanding and wisdom. Help me trust you completely today.

AMEN

you can
totally do
this

He who finds a wife finds what is good and receives favor from the LORD.
Proverbs 18:22

As you spend time with God today, write down the things He shares with you as He shows you how to love your wife.

_____

_____

_____

_____

_____

_____

_____

_____

_____

_____

_____

_____

_____

_____

_____

_____

Use these lines to record God's faithfulness.

_____

_____

_____

_____

_____

_____

_____

_____

_____

_____

_____

_____

_____

_____

_____

_____

Above all else, guard your heart, for it is the wellspring
of life. Proverbs 4:23

11

Tools to grow your Love

Guard Your Thoughts

Be careful of the thoughts you think about your wife. If they are not positive or team building, throw those thoughts away. Your thoughts will affect your actions. Guard your mind and only invite good thoughts to stay. Your love skills are growing!

Adam and Monica had only been married 9 months, when Monica decided she wanted out of their marriage. She did not think Adam respected her or treasured who she was. Monica told Adam she wanted a divorce and that made him, angrier. Adam became desperate, so he decided to talk with their local minister. They had not been attending regularly but, he needed help sorting out some issues they were having.

As Adam met with Pastor White, he told the minister, Monica believed he did not love her.

12

He sat for 1 ½ hours telling this minister how much he loved and valued his wife. When he was finished, Pastor White looked at him and said, "Young man if you can tell her what you just told me with your actions, you will never get divorced." The minister then shared with Adam some things he needed to work on with his wife. The minister told him,

1. Make her feel treasured and loved.
2. Watch everything you think. Guard your thoughts with purpose-filled intention, inviting only good thoughts to stay.
3. Keep God at the center of your marriage and relationship. Without God, you will not make it. With God anything is possible.
4. Attend church regularly and grow together with God.
5. Treat her better than you did when you were dating and trying to win her heart.
6. Take your role as a husband seriously and place a high value on the heart God has entrusted to you!
7. Keep sin out of your heart and marriage!
8. Be quick to say you are sorry, even when you feel you are right.

As Adam listened to the minister, he decided to practice daily, living with the tools Pastor White had given him. When he got home that day, he told Monica he loved her more than the air he was breathing.

Adam made every attempt to show her love through his actions. This amazing couple began attending church regularly. When Adam and Monica got home, they would discuss the sermon and the many things they had heard that day.

No matter where your marriage is at, you can change your marital course and turn it around like you do a ship in the ocean with the proper navigation. Remember to focus on only good thoughts and throw your negative thoughts away!

On the lines below, record your good thoughts about your wife. Remember what you feed will grow! Keep feeding your good thoughts and they will grow!

My good thoughts about my marriage and wife are

_____

_____

_____

_____

_____

_____

_____

_____

_____

_____

_____

_____

_____

_____

Good thoughts will grow my love for my wife!

Your positive thoughts entertain God's goodness!

YOUR MIND WILL OVERFLOW
WITH LOVE THOUGHTS

God hovers over you with answers to the questions that lay upon your heart.

_____

_____

_____

_____

_____

_____

_____

_____

_____

_____

_____

_____

_____

_____

_____

_____

Use these lines to record God's faithfulness.

_____

_____

_____

_____

_____

_____

_____

_____

_____

_____

_____

_____

_____

_____

_____

_____

A gentle answer turns away wrath, but a harsh word stirs up anger. Proverbs 15:1

Tools to grow your love

Guard Your Words

Stand guard over the words you speak about your wife. There is power in your words and you will find yourself creating a world you live in with your words. Speak good and positive things about your wife. As you become aware of the things you speak, you will be amazed at how your words affect your world. If you say your wife does not love you that is fruit you will be eating! If you say she does not respect you, she will not.

Charlie and Allison had been married 6 months. Charlie had a good job working for the city and Allison stayed home to cook and clean. After they had been married 3 months, Charlie noticed, Allison had not gone grocery shopping, the supper was not ready when he got home, and

19

the house always looked like a tornado had hit it. He came home one day feeling down when he saw the condition of their house. He decided to take Allison out to eat and talk to her.

As they sat waiting on their food, Charlie looked at her and told her he wanted to share some things with her. Allison looked back at him, giving Charlie her full attention. Charlie said, "I first need to tell you, I love you! You matter more to me than the paycheck I bring home every week." Allison felt tears forming in her eyes. Charlie was not finished though. He looked at her and said, "I want to apologize to you for taking you for granted." You cooked, cleaned, always had the food on the table, and instead of appreciating you, I expected your service." Allison's face became wet with tears, as she sat there unable to believe he was somehow able to figure out how she was feeling.

He looked at her and said, "My love, every Friday, is going to be our date night. You do not have to fix supper and have it on the table. I am going to take you out as a way of expressing my gratitude to you for cooking all week." The two held hands as they sat beside each other in the restaurant booth. Charlie could have accused Allison of being lazy, but instead he chose to build her with his words and use understanding with his heart.

Today take the time to build your wife and tell her all the many ways she blesses you. If you do not think she respects you, tell her you are blessed to have a wife that honors and respects you. Do not say this with sarcasm but, be sincere and speak with a heart of total sincerity. God loves you both and His heart is for you! God will give you the words to speak to your wife. He enjoys the way you love her well!

On the following lines, record good things about your wife, as you speak and declare good things over her!

My wife is

_____

_____

_____

_____

_____

_____

_____

_____

_____

_____

_____

_____

_____

_____

_____

Create a world of beauty with
your love words!

> *Your ability to choose
> your words carefully
> will make you wise!*

YOUR WORDS
are healing
AND SEASONED
with my
GRACE

Inhale God's presence today as you feel Him hovering over you. He has all the answers you need!

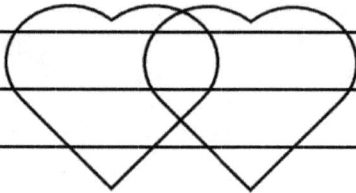

_____
_____
_____
_____
_____
_____
_____
_____
_____
_____
_____
_____
_____
_____
_____
_____
_____

Use these lines to record God's faithfulness.

_____

_____

_____

_____

_____

_____

_____

_____

_____

_____

_____

_____

_____

_____

_____

_____

My dear brothers, take note of this: Everyone should be quick to listen, slow to speak and slow to become angry, James 1:19

Tools to grow your love

Listen Well

Listen to your wife with the intent to understand her. Be careful not to listen just to answer her. This is a priceless tool that will grow your love. You will find your understanding growing as you focus on listening to her heart. Utilizing the tool of listening daily will make you wise! Keep nurturing your love!

Jack and Jill had dated for 5 years before they decided to get married. They had their problems like every couple, but they decided to jump off that marital bridge and just do it!

Three months after they had gotten married, Jill decided she did not want to be married anymore! She told Jack, she was done and wanted out. Jack was baffled and could not believe what he was hearing. "Why?" he asked her. She replied, "You do not hear me when I talk, and you never listen to what I am saying. You do not value me as a person enough to listen to my heart." Jack could not believe what he was hearing. He stood there and apologized to Jill but, she did not want anything to do with his empty words. Her heart was filled with meaningless apologies that had not been followed with love actions.

Jack left that night, but decided he was not giving up on their marriage. He sat down and began to meditate on everything Jill had told him. He knew if they were going to succeed in their marriage, he needed to make some changes!

That night Jack prayed and asked God for His help with their marriage. He asked God to forgive him for not being faithful in church and praying with his wife. As Jack sat quietly before God, he found his heart filled with God's peace and love! He then wrote a love letter to Jill, thanking her for marrying him. He also told her everything he appreciated about her. Jack ended the letter with all the things he had done that he was sorry for. Jill read the letter and decided she needed to forgive her husband and give him another chance.

Jack asked her if she would go to church with him on Sunday. She agreed and this young couple started attending church together regularly. They found peace within both their hearts as they prayed before they left the house.

Jack and Jill filled their nights with prayers to God and fun activities during the day. They created memories for years to come! This young couple beat the odds as they moved past what had happened and embraced their future together with God.

As a husband your role is important to God. He will show you daily, how to love your wife. *On the lines below write out the many ways you can listen to the heart of your wife to a greater degree.*

I can listen to the heart of my wife by,

_____

_____

_____

_____

_____

_____

_____

_____

_____

_____

_____

_____

_____

_____

_____

_____

_____

_____

_____

Listening will help me understand my wife!

The act of listening is an amazing way to love your wife!

you will hear love

THROUGH MY HEART

your response

WILL

be transforming

Enjoy God's goodness today, as He shows you how your wife needs to be loved today.

_____
_____
_____
_____
_____
_____
_____
_____
_____
_____
_____
_____
_____
_____
_____
_____
_____

Use these lines to record God's faithfulness.

_____

_____

_____

_____

_____

_____

_____

_____

_____

_____

_____

_____

_____

_____

_____

_____

_____

_____

Husbands, love your wives, just as Christ loved the
church and gave himself up for her.   Ephesians 5:25

Tools to grow your love

Be Thoughtful

Thinking about your wife when you are apart will grow your love. A simple love text at lunch or a phone call when you get off work to see if she needs anything will remind her, that she is forever in your heart! God enjoys the way you love each other!

Brian and Betty had dated 3 ½ years when Betty decided she wanted to date other people. Brian had proposed to her and he genuinely loved her. When he asked her, why she wanted to see other people, she basically told him, she did not feel like he thought about her or valued her. She told him she could not get married when he did not treasure her when they were just dating! She asked for some time apart and he willingly gave it to her. They both took time apart to search their souls. Brian asked God to help him love Betty in a greater way.

As Brian prayed daily, he found God laying things on his heart, showing him how to love Betty. The quietness in God's presence became almost overwhelming as he listened to God lay things on his heart and show him how she needed to be loved! Brian sent Betty text messages during the day with a prayer and a scripture God had laid on his heart for her. He put a love letter in the mail and thanked her for being his best friend.

This amazing couple got back together, planned their wedding and if you were to ask them today how they did it, they would say, "With God." As a husband your role to God is important. He longs to lay things on your heart and show you daily how to love your wife!

On the lines below write out the many ways you can be more thoughtful!

_____

_____

_____

_____

_____

_____

_____

_____

_____

_____

_____

_____

_____

*Your thoughtfulness will grow
your love!*

*Your thoughtfulness will
create memories for years
to come!*

I HAVE CALLED YOU TO

BE

A STRONG LEADER

FOR RIGHTEOUSNESS

As you spend time with God today, write out the things He shares with you as He shows you how to love your wife.

_____

_____

_____

_____

_____

_____

_____

_____

_____

_____

_____

_____

_____

_____

_____

_____

Use these lines to record God's faithfulness.

_____

_____

_____

_____

_____

_____

_____

_____

_____

_____

_____

_____

_____

_____

_____

_____

_____

For in the same way you judge others, you will be judged, and with the measure you use, it will be measured to you. Matthew 7:2

38

Tools to grow your love

Do Not Judge

Throw away judgment and be careful of finger pointing. Focus on the positives and choose to love. Just flip the switch and instead of focusing on the bad, focus on the good. You will find judgment destroying your marriage and other relationships. Daily guard against finger-pointing! Your love is growing!

Alex and Alissa had been married 2 months. They were high school sweethearts and got along well with each other. This couple found a small house within their budget close to their work commute. They settled into the strong red brick house, they both decided to buy.

Six months after they were married, they

began to struggle relationally. Alex could not understand why Alissa's mom was so judgmental. Alex discussed his feelings with Alissa, and she defended her mother. This loving couple ended up in a place, bankrupt of love. They no longer thought good things about each other but found themselves being judgmental and unforgiving.

Alex prayed and asked God for His help. He knew if things were to work, it would be a miracle from God! Alex went to bed that night feeling God's love fill his heart. He asked God to forgive him for being judgmental toward his wife's family.

That next day, Alex apologized to Alissa. He asked her to forgive him for judging her family. Alissa got tears in her eyes, as she felt the sincerity of the words Alex spoke. They hugged one another and began to fill the heart of each other with genuine love from God.

They both decided they needed to attend church regularly and make God the center of their marriage. They began to pray together daily. This amazing couple used their words to bless each other and their family that surrounded them.

No matter what situation you find yourself in, there is always hope with God! Today take the time to search your hearts to see if there is any area in your heart, where you have judged someone else. When you judge others, you will find yourself opening the door for judgment to come into your marriage! Take the time to exchange judgment for love.

Speak blessings over the people you may have judged!
I bless

_____
_____
_____
_____
_____
_____
_____
_____
_____
_____

I choose to guard my heart
from judgment!

Look for opportunities to think the best about your wife!

YOUR FAITH TRANSFORMS ENVIRONMENTS

God hovers over you with answers to the questions that lay upon your heart.

_____

_____

_____

_____

_____

_____

_____

_____

_____

_____

_____

_____

_____

_____

_____

_____

Use these lines to record God's faithfulness.

_____

_____

_____

_____

_____

_____

_____

_____

_____

_____

_____

_____

_____

_____

_____

_____

He has made everything beautiful in its time. He has also set eternity in the hearts of men; yet they can not fathom what God has done from beginning to end. Ecclesiastes 3:11

Tools to grow your Love

Value Time

Value every moment together, the good and the bad. Time moves and cannot be stopped and once the moment is gone, you cannot get it back! Learn from the bad, increase the good and value your time together as precious and priceless! This will make you wise! God has given us time and learning to value and appreciate the time He has given us is priceless!

Barry and Benita had been married for 15 years. They loved each other and enjoyed spending time together. Their friends and loved ones looked forward to hanging with them, as they expressed their love to each other. This awesome couple enjoyed date nights together as they reminisced over happy times that had brought them both joy!

Benita had created a value book of all their dates and happy times together. If they went to the movies, she would put the stubs of their tickets in her value book. On their 15th wedding anniversary, Benita gave Barry the book she had been making. Barry did not know about the book and when he saw it, his heart was moved. He knew his wife loved him, but to value, the time they had spent together with every penny, increased his gratitude for his wife.

Benita had to work over one Friday night, but she called Barry and told him she would meet him at the restaurant at 6:00 pm. Barry waited patiently at the restaurant. He was there 3 hours, when he finally decided he would go home. He tried to reach Benita on her phone, but she did not answer. When he got home, he found his lovely, beautiful wife, on the floor. She was barely hanging on. Barry did not know it at the time, but his remarkable wife had suffered a heart attack and was hanging onto life with only a thread of hope. Barry ran for the phone when he saw his wife.

It did not take the emergency team exceptionally long to get to their house. They gave Benita oxygen, put an IV in her arm and headed for the local hospital. Once they arrived at the General Hospital, Barry found himself saying, "Goodbye." His wife had lost the strength to hold on, and she had slipped away. Barry did not want to let go of her cold hand. He found his heart grateful for every moment they had spent together.

As he drove home by himself that night, he found his soul full of sadness at losing his one and only. His heart was grateful for valuing every moment with this beautiful woman who was now gone.

On the lines below record the many ways your value for time has affected your outlook on circumstances and situations

_____
_____
_____
_____
_____
_____
_____

_____

_____

_____

_____

_____

_____

_____

_____

_____

_____

*As I value time, I will add value to
my marriage and relationship!*

*Your choice to treasure every
moment will make you wise
beyond your years!*

YOU WILL KNOW ME AS
YOUR ABBA FATHER

Inhale God's presence today as you feel Him hovering over you. He has all the answers you need!

_____

_____

_____

_____

_____

_____

_____

_____

_____

_____

_____

_____

_____

_____

_____

Use these lines to record God's faithfulness.

But just as you excel in everything, in faith, in speech, in knowledge, in complete earnestness and in your love for us, see that you also excel in this grace of giving.
II Corinthians 8:7

Tools to grow your love

Be Excellent

Excel at being a husband. You can just be married, have a marriage certificate, or excel at being the best. When you chose to live above average and mediocrity, you will reap the rewards of your excellence! Your distinction in supremacy will make a difference in the lives around you! Excellence is your birthright! Heaven is watching and cheering for you!

Lee and Brianne had been married for 2 years. They enjoyed each other, their lives together and their date nights every week. Lee had been in the Navy and he had developed a few traits that Brianne admired. He always seemed to portray the need to be perfect.

Although he knew he was not perfect, he always carried the expectation for himself to be excellent. This character trait caused him to value Brianne and treat her with superb niceness. Lee had also received a promotion at work for his excellence. He came home that night to share the good news with Brianne. This couple took the night off and went to Lee's favorite restaurant to celebrate his success. Lee lived life with excellence and his superbness affected every area of his life. His excellence had a huge impact on Brianne.

Today think about the many ways your excellence could affect your wife, your marriage, and your life!

_____

_____

_____

_____

_____

_____

_____

_____

_____

List other areas your excellence will affect!

1._____

2._____

3._____

4._____

5._____

6._____

7._____

Your excellence will transform your world!

> Giving my best will reap huge rewards!

VICTORY IS
in your
HAND

Enjoy God's goodness today, as He shows you how your wife needs to be loved today.

_____

_____

_____

_____

_____

_____

_____

_____

_____

_____

_____

_____

_____

_____

_____

_____

Use these lines to record God's faithfulness.

_____

_____

_____

_____

_____

_____

_____

_____

_____

_____

_____

_____

_____

_____

_____

Words from a wise man's mouth are gracious, but a fool is consumed by his own lips. Ecclesiastes 10:12

Tools to grow your love

Use Love Phrases

Find love phrases or words you can give your wife to express your love. Your verbal expression of love is just as important as your actions. Your love words will nurture your relationship and grow your love. God enjoys the way you love your wife!

Nick and Nautica had dated 2 years before they decided to say, "I do." They were surrounded by family and friends, both near and far. They had been planning this day for 1 ½ years. It did not take them long to realize they were a perfect fit. Nick would remind Nautica daily that she completed him, and Nautica would remind Nick that she was in love for the first time in her life! The love between this amazing couple grew. Others around them were blessed to be in their circle as they experienced the love exchange between these love birds.

Nick grew their love using romantic phrases with his wife and choosing to build her daily. Today take the time to think of love phrases you can give your wife daily. Remember when you talk, you are feeding her spirit. As you daily feed her good words, you will find your love growing! God enjoys the way you love your wife!

Take the time to think about some love phrases that will nurture your wife's heart!

_____

_____

_____

_____

_____

_____

_____

_____

_____

_____

_____

_____

_____

_____

_____

_____

_____

_____

_____

The goodness you feed your wife,
will grow your love!

Your thoughtfulness
will create memories
for years to come!

MY LIGHT
IS SEEN IN
AND
THROUGH
YOU

*As you spend time with God today,
write down the things He shares with you
as He shows you how to love your wife.*

_____

_____

_____

_____

_____

_____

_____

_____

_____

_____

_____

_____

_____

_____

_____

_____

Use these lines to record God's faithfulness.

_____

_____

_____

_____

_____

_____

_____

_____

_____

_____

_____

_____

_____

_____

_____

_____

Drink water from your own cistern, running water from your own well. Proverbs 5:15

Tools to grow your love

Notice Your Wife

Use your eyes to notice your wife. Be ready to pick her up with God words when she is having an off day. Your faithful loving support through her hard days will nurture your relationship. God is faithful in noticing you and He loves the way you notice your wife.

Brandon and Brittney had been married 3 years. They both worked the same shift, and they enjoyed their long conversations in the evenings as they discussed the unexpected events of their day. Tuesday when Brandon came home, he noticed his wife was not in the kitchen fixing supper. He called for her and when he went into their bedroom, he found her in bed, wiping her face, as she tried to hide her tears. Brandon sat on the edge of the bed and asked her what was wrong. His compassion and care caused her tears to increase, running down her face.

She could not hide her disappointment. She looked at him and said, "Baby I was laid off today." He looked at her and said, "What?" He told her he was grateful she was fine. Brandon was glad she was not sick. He knew the news she shared with him could have been a lot worse.

Brandon took Brittney out that night and encouraged her over good food and uplifting words. He reminded her that she had a lot to offer other firms and landing a good job would not be hard for her. He said a prayer with her that night before they went to bed. When Brittney woke up the following morning, she found her heart full of hope. Brandon not only noticed his wife, but he was there to give her encouraging words and remind her that he knew things could have been a lot worse.

Your role as a husband is important to God and He longs for you to love your wife like He loves you. Today think of ways you can notice your wife to a greater level. *On the lines below, list the many ways, you can notice her in a greater way.* **God notices you and He enjoys the way you notice your wife.**

I noticed my wife

_____

_____

_____

_____

_____

_____

_____

_____

When my wife is feeling low, I will

_____

_____

_____

_____

_____

_____

_____

_____

_____

_____

_____

_____

_____

_____

_____

_____

My wife is a precious gift from God, I enjoy!

Noticing your wife is another way of loving her well!

I enjoy the
WAY YOU
love your
—— WIFE! ——
It brings great
JOY TO MY
HEART!

God hovers over you with answers to the questions that lay upon your heart.

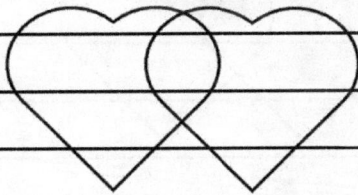

Use these lines to record God's faithfulness.

_____

_____

_____

_____

_____

_____

_____

_____

_____

_____

_____

_____

_____

_____

_____

_____

Give thanks in all circumstances, for this is God's will for you in Christ Jesus. I Thessalonians 5:18

Tools to grow your love

Be Thankful

Always carry a heart of thanksgiving. Cultivating a heart of gratitude will nurture your love. When you could complain and you choose to be thankful, you will find your love growing with your thanksgiving. Stay grateful and keep growing your love!

Kyle and Karen had been married 1 ½ years. They both had suffered tragedy through life and found their hearts grateful for everything and each other. When Kyle was 10, he had lost his mother to a battling disease of cancer. She passed away 5 days before his eleventh birthday. Although Kyle recalls it as a hard time, he would tell you today, that he found gold though the tragedy.

The gold he found was gratitude. He lost

his mother, but he was determined to be grateful for everyone and everything. His friends found themselves blessed to know him, and his wife was just as grateful. Karen enjoyed their conversations about Kyle's mother and the gold, Kyle felt he had gained from it. Karen did not realize the depts of Kyle's gratitude until they got married. If Karen fixed his lunch, he would call and thank her for his amazing lunch. If she mowed the grass, swept the carpets, or went grocery shopping, he was always verbalizing his gratitude to her for everything she did.

Karen realized one day; she was not as grateful as Kyle. She knew she took things for granted and she decided to be more verbal and expressive with her gratitude like her awesome husband. That next day, when Kyle came home and told Karen he had filled her car up with gas, she verbally expressed her gratitude. Kyle and Karen grew their love with their gratitude.

Kyle could have been an average husband who took Karen's duties as a wife for granted. He chose to grow their love with his gratitude. His gratitude made an inspirational impact on his wife. She in return decided to be more grateful. Together this amazing couple made an impact on each other and those around them. As a husband your role is important. God is with you on this awesome love journey.

Today take time to meditate on the many things you are grateful for. Keep growing your gratitude!

1._____

2._____

3._____

4._____

5._____

Practicing your gratitude skills daily, will change your life!

I HAVE GIVEN
you courage and
YOU WILL NOT FEAR
but will face
AND CONQUER

Inhale God's presence today as you feel Him hovering over you. He has all the answers you need!

_____

_____

_____

_____

_____

_____

_____

_____

_____

_____

_____

_____

_____

_____

_____

_____

Use these lines to record God's faithfulness.

_____

_____

_____

_____

_____

_____

_____

_____

_____

_____

_____

_____

_____

_____

_____

_____

_____

_____

For if you forgive men when they sin against you, your
heavenly Father will also forgive you.   Matthew 6:14

Tools to grow your Love

Let Go

Do not hang on to offenses. Choose to live everyday with the tool of forgiveness. You will find yourself carrying offenses from days, into weeks into months into the following year without the grace of forgiveness. Don't expect perfection from your wife. Just love and let grace grow within your heart! **Heaven is cheering you on!**

Mark and Maria had been married for 5 years. If you met them, you would have thought they were newlyweds. They were expressive with their love and gratitude to each other for even the little things. Mark had been married before and when it was finalized, he could not even remember why they had started fighting. His friends at work one day asked him if she was running around on him and he responded with, "No." They looked at him and said, "Why did you get divorced?" Mark still remembers that day, as he stumbled around for an explanation. All he could remember was their fighting and the inability to get along.

When it was all over, Mark decided he needed to forgive everyone for everything. He brought this concept into his marriage with Maria and it had a huge impact on their relationship and their friends. If Mark could talk to you today, he would tell you to forgive everyone for everything. He had a huge impact on his wife and those that knew him.

Today take time to search your heart for anything you might need to let go of. When you hang on to offenses with people in your life, your heart will automatically hang on to offenses with your wife. Learning to let go is a tool that will help nurture your marriage and relationships with others. As you display the ability to forgive your wife and those in your life, you will find yourself leaving a huge impact on your wife! Life is short and living with the tool of forgiveness, is living well!

On the Lines below list the many things you are letting go of.

I am letting go of,

_____

_____

_____

_____

_____

_____

_____

_____

I choose to forgive, to grow my love!

> *Letting go is a needed essential for the success of marriage!*

you are an
OVERCOMER AND YOUR
ENEMY KNOWS
where you step

Enjoy God's goodness today, as He shows you how your wife needs to be loved.

_____

_____

_____

_____

_____

_____

_____

_____

_____

_____

_____

_____

_____

_____

_____

_____

Use these lines to record God's faithfulness.

_____

_____

_____

_____

_____

_____

_____

_____

_____

_____

_____

_____

_____

_____

_____

_____

_____

_____

For I know my transgressions, and my sin is always
before me. Psalm 51:3

Tools to grow your love

Stay Humble

When you disappoint your wife or let her down, be quick to apologize. When you are quick and ready to apologize, it does not make you weak but strong in God. God loves your humility. As you continue to plant seeds of humility, you will reap a harvest of goodness.

Aaron and Amy had only been married 7 months. They worked opposite shifts and found love moments through texts and love notes they left for each other. Aaron's parents had gotten divorced when he was young and he felt like a wise man, as he learned from the mistakes they had made. As a child growing up, he never heard his father apologize to his mother, even when he was wrong. He knew this had created problems for his parent's marriage and his relationship with his dad.

When Aaron got older, he decided he would always stay humble by apologizing even when he thought he was right. Amy loved the way Aaron honored and respected her. If he thought she was upset about something, he wanted to talk about it which always ended in an apology. No matter what your childhood, or environment has been, you can learn humility and chose to honor others in your life. Aaron learned from others in his life. He chose to live well for his wife and their children.

Today take time to search your heart for areas you might need to increase humility. God loves your humility and your ability to give Him all honor, brings great joy to His heart!

Practice your humility on the following lines and grow your love!

I will apologize to my wife when

_____

_____

_____

I will practice humility by

_____

_____

_____

_____

_____

_____

_____

**My humility reflects my love
for God and my wife!**

*I will remind myself it
is not just about me!*

YOU WILL
KNOW ME
THROUGH
ENCOUNTERING
ME

*As you spend time with God today,
write down the things He shares with you
as He shows you how to love your wife.*

Use these lines to record God's faithfulness.

_____

_____

_____

_____

_____

_____

_____

_____

_____

_____

_____

_____

_____

_____

_____

_____

_____

_____

_____

A hot-tempered man stirs up dissension, but a patient man calms a quarrel. Proverbs 15:18

Tools to grow your love

Don't Be a Right Fighter

Guard against being a right fighter. Remember you are on the same team. Focus on working together more than who is right. You will find your love growing as you nurture your ability to be a team. God enjoys your teamwork.

Bruce and Cecelia had been married for 14 months. Bruce was a fire fighter and Cecelia worked as an EMT. Both of their jobs required teamwork with others and they both brought their teamwork spirit into their marriage and home. There was nothing they enjoyed more than working together as a team. This amazing couple worked side by side on everything. If

Cecelia needed to go to the store for groceries; Bruce was always willing to drive her. The team spirit of this young couple had a huge impact on their neighbors and those around them.

Bruce had watched his brother Eugene be a right fighter. It did not matter what he was doing, he was always right. Eugene's attitude had affected his marriage. He was divorced, bitter and had a bad attitude toward life. Bruce had decided he was not going to be like Eugene. If Bruce and Cecelia had a disagreement, he would work hard to see her side of things. Cecelia loved Bruce for his flexibility and willingness to always be a team. Bruce was committed to his wife and their marriage. His ability to be flexible even when he thought he was right had an influential impression on his beautiful wife.

Today take time to think about your responses when you disagree with your wife. Do you always have to be right? You can be a man of honor without being a right fighter. Remember, it is not all about you.

On the lines below list the things you can change, to help you respond to your wife in a better manner!

To keep from being a right fighter, I will...

_____
_____
_____
_____
_____
_____
_____
_____

I will remember I do not always need to be right!

The ability to be right does not define my manhood!

YOU WILL
BE
KNOWN
AS A MAN OF
GREAT
COURAGE

God hovers over you with answers to the questions that lay upon your heart.

_____

_____

_____

_____

_____

_____

_____

_____

_____

_____

_____

_____

_____

_____

Use these lines to record God's faithfulness.

_____

_____

_____

_____

_____

_____

_____

_____

_____

_____

_____

_____

_____

_____

_____

Give, and it will be given unto you. A good measure, pressed down, shaken together and running over, will be poured into your lap. For with the measure you use, it will be measured to you. Luke 6:38

Tools to grow your love

Be A Giver

Cultivate a heart of giving. When you live with the attribute to give, it will have a huge impact on your marriage and life. Giving will suffocate selfishness. Give your time, heart, and love to God first, then your wife!

Malek was raised in an environment of giving. His parents had taught him to think about others and to always put people around him above himself. He had learned to live and model those attributes. When Mica met Malek, she loved him for his kindness toward her, strangers, and others in their lives. They began to date, and it did not take long for them to get married. They went regularly to their local church and Malek gave his tithe, time and service to God, His wife, and others. Mica was always beside him as a loyal supporter, loving him and admiring his willingness to give. Malek and Mica grew their love and devotion to each other with the attribute of giving. As a husband, he found his giving growing their love and nurturing the heart of his wife.

As a husband you will receive multiple opportunities daily to think about yourself first, or to put your wife above your own wants and desires. You will find cultivating the skill of giving in your marriage, to be a priceless tool.

Today, take some time to think about the many ways you can give to a greater level! Learning to give is an amazing tool that will grow your love!

I can practice giving by

_____

_____

_____

_____

_____

_____

_____

_____

_____

_____

_____

_____

_____

_____

_____

_____

Giving will grow my love!

Giving is a supernatural door opener that will bless you with more!

You will crush your enemy
under your foot

Inhale God's presence today as you feel Him hovering over you. He has all the answers you need!

_____

_____

_____

_____

_____

_____

_____

_____

_____

_____

_____

_____

_____

_____

_____

_____

Use these lines to record God's faithfulness.

_____

_____

_____

_____

_____

_____

_____

_____

_____

_____

_____

_____

_____

_____

In the same way, husbands ought to love their wives as their own bodies. He who loves his wife loves himself. Ephesians 5:28

100

Tools to grow your love

Make a full investment

Invest fully in your marriage. Put your heart and soul into your relationship and love your wife fully. She will know when you are emotionally connected and when she feels your investment, she will feel secure in your marriage. Keep growing your love!

Samuel and Sarah had been married 2 years. They dated a while before they got married and although they worked in different cities, they still managed to love each other well. They synched their schedules so they could meet for lunch on Fridays. Sarah always looked forward to their lunch dates. She would get to see her one and only and hear all about his amazing day. Samuel was totally in love with Sarah and everyone he worked with knew how amazing she was. This couple was committed to each other, their marriage and growing their love.

Samuel utilized every opportunity to show Sarah he was totally committed to her and their marriage. He had eyes and a heart for only his wife, and she knew it. Like Samuel and Sarah, you can grow your love and be totally committed to each other.

Today, think about the impact your full investment would have on your marriage. Make a list of the things you can change to invest fully in your marriage!

To be totally invested in my marriage I can change...

_____

_____

_____

_____

_____

_____

_____

_____

_____

_____

_____

_____

_____

_____

_____

_____

*Making a total investment in
my marriage is wise!*

*Your wife will know when you
are totally invested! Stay
committed and grow your love!*

YOU
are the
HEAD AND
not
THE TAIL,
above and
NOT BENEATH

Enjoy God's goodness today, as He shows you how your wife needs to be loved today.

_____

_____

_____

_____

_____

_____

_____

_____

_____

_____

_____

_____

_____

_____

Use these lines to record God's faithfulness.

_____

_____

_____

_____

_____

_____

_____

_____

_____

_____

_____

_____

_____

_____

_____

_____

_____

_____

Each of you should look not only to your own interests, but also to the interests of others. Philippians 2:4

Tools to grow your love

Consider the Timing

Timing is everything. Even though you may be upset or bothered by something, it might not be the right place or time to discuss it. Be wise and show your consideration by waiting for the right time to discuss your concerns. Keep nurturing your love.

Isaiah and Isabella were in love. They had been married 3 years and to meet them, you would have thought they were newlyweds. This couple had been high school sweethearts and they loved being together no matter what they were doing.

Isaiah worked as a police officer and Isabella worked in the school office. They both loved their work as they served others. Isaiah had learned at work, that timing was everything. Isabella had also applied this wisdom to her occupation. Together this amazing couple knew the importance of timing. If they were miffed about something that had happened between them, they would always consider the timing. Isaiah and Isabella were not only married, but best friends. Their consideration for each other when they were upset grew their love.

Isaiah knew the significance of timing. He used this priceless tool in their marriage to grow their love. As a husband, you will be given opportunities to vent whenever you feel the need or to consider the timing of your concerns. It is important to remember, sowing consideration into your marriage will allow you to reap it in return. Your wife will feel your love and your consideration will grow your love!

Today take time to think about your timing skills. Praying when you are upset and giving God your thoughts and feelings can grow your love! It is important to remember, that timing is everything.

On the lines below list the many ways you can increase your timing skills.
I can increase my timing skills by,

_____

_____

_____

_____

_____

_____

_____

_____

_____

_____

**I will work on being
considerate of my wife when I
need to discuss issues
that trouble me!**

*Your considerate timing
will grow your love!
Your love skills are*

MY HEAVEN'S
WILL BE OPENED
TO YOU AND
YOU WILL
RECEIVE DIVINE
INSPIRATION
TO SOLVE PROBLEMS

As you spend time with God today, write down the things He shares with you as He shows you how to love your wife.

_____

_____

_____

_____

_____

_____

_____

_____

_____

_____

_____

_____

_____

_____

Use these lines to record God's faithfulness.

_____

_____

_____

_____

_____

_____

_____

_____

_____

_____

_____

_____

_____

_____

_____

_____

_____

_____

_____

_____

My commandment is this: Love each other as I have loved you. John 15:12

112

Tools to grow your love

Compromise

Now that you are married, think about your wife. Remember the world does not revolve around you. Work on being flexible and creating compromise even when you want your own way. Your flexibility will grow your love.

Noah and Natali had been married 3 years. Their love seemed to grow with every day and month that passed. Noah was raised in a family with 5 brothers and 4 sisters. He had learned the jewel of compromise and he had brought this wisdom into their marriage. Natali was a corporate executive, and it was her job to hear the voices of all the employees and implement positive changes to save the company money. Natali had not only learned the important traits of compromise at work but, from her loving husband Noah. Natali felt wise as she compromised at home with Noah. You could probably almost consider it a love war when Noah wanted to go to Natali's favorite restaurant and Natali wanted to visit Noah's wished-for restaurant. This amazing couple loved each other so well, their friends and neighbors felt blessed to have such an amazing love couple in their lives. Noah's compromise had a huge impact on his wife.

As a husband you will find the best way to bring change into your marriage is through your actions. Today think about all the ways you can compromise. Even though you might have a strong opinion about things, learn to think about the feelings of your wife. Your compromise will grow your love and cherish the heart of your one and only!

On the lines below list the many ways you can compromise and increase your thoughtfulness. Your love skills are amazing!

I can utilize the skill of compromise in my marriage by,

_____

_____

_____

_____

_____

_____

I can be more thoughtful and think about my wife by,

_____

_____

_____

_____

Compromise will grow our marital love and thoughtfulness for each other!

IT IS MY GOODNESS YOU SEE SURROUNDING YOU!

God hovers over you with answers to the questions that lay upon your heart.

_____

_____

_____

_____

_____

_____

_____

_____

_____

_____

_____

_____

_____

_____

_____

_____

Use these lines to record God's faithfulness.

_____

_____

_____

_____

_____

_____

_____

_____

_____

_____

_____

_____

_____

_____

_____

_____

So I recommend the enjoyment of life, because nothing is better for a man under the sun than to eat and drink and be glad. Then joy will accompany him in his work all the days of the life God has given him under the sun.
Ecclesiastes 8:15

Tools to grow your love

Find the Fun

Focus on making your marriage an adventure. Be spontaneous, adventurous, plan at times and always engage in your love life together with gratitude for each other. Embracing the unexpected with fun, will create memories for tomorrow. Your love skills are amazing!

Jim and Lassie celebrated their 1-year anniversary filled with fun and love. They always had a way of finding pleasure in everything they did. They both got up that morning packed a bag and headed toward the beach. Today would mark a first for both of them. They rented a boat and headed out into the ocean waters. The sky was clear, and it seemed as if it was going to be a beautiful day. The waves were huge as they splashed up against their sailboat, tossing them further out into the ocean. Jim and Lassie enjoyed the warm bright sun on the deck; then they went below to enjoy each other. They spent the day out on the refreshing sea. When the sun went down, they turned the boat around to head toward shore.

This young couple knew how to have fun, work hard, and enjoy every moment. When they reached the shore, Lassie needed a love moment with Jim to thank him for the beautiful day he had planned for them. Jim not only knew how to work hard, but how to have fun. His ability to pull the plug and enjoy the day with his beautiful wife, grew their love! This amazing couple found the fun in marriage to be totally energizing!

Today take some time to think about the many things you can do to bring adventure and fun into your relationship! Using every opportunity to lead with fun and adventure will grow your love!

List all the God thoughts He gives you on the lines below!
I can be more spontaneous and adventurous by,

_____

_____

_____

_____

_____

_____

_____

_____

_____

_____

Finding the fun in marriage and life is totally energizing!

The Fun in marriage will nurture your souls and grow your love!

you will FiND REST in ME

Inhale God's presence today as you feel Him hovering over you. He has all the answers you need!

_____

_____

_____

_____

_____

_____

_____

_____

_____

_____

_____

_____

_____

_____

_____

_____

_____

Use these lines to record God's faithfulness.

_____

_____

_____

_____

_____

_____

_____

_____

_____

_____

_____

_____

_____

_____

_____

_____

Do everything in love. I Corinthians 16:14

Tools to grow your love

Learn to Engage

When your wife discusses things, you have no interest in, focus on engaging her. Hearing about a bargain on nail polish, or the latest fashion on shoes might not appeal to you. When she is talking about her latest bargain, engaging with her will nurture her heart! Listening to the heart of your wife will allow you to deepen your understanding of her. This will grow your love and nurture your marriage. This is a priceless tool to practice!

Kyle and Candice were newlyweds. Kyle was a therapist and Candice worked as a cashier at the local supermarket. They both had their schedules synched, so they could spend their evenings together. They enjoyed their late-night conversations about events that had taken place throughout the day. Kyle was a therapist and he had learned to focus on what others were saying when they were speaking. This was a characteristic he utilized at home with his loving wife. If he found himself bored or uninterested in what Candice was talking about, he would focus more on what she was saying. He had learned the importance of listening with the intent to understand what the other person was saying. Kyle knew when his wife was speaking, she was concerned about something.

Candice had also learned to listen to Kyle. This was something she had learned from her husband. This amazing couple utilized the ability to listen to each other to grow their love and understand the heart of each other.

As a husband your example of listening to the heart of your wife will be an influential game changer. Today, look for opportunities where you can seek to understand the heart of your wife in a greater way.

On the following lines list, the many things you can do to engage with your wife in a greater way. God loves the way you love your wife!

I can engage with my wife in a greater way by,

_____

_____

_____

_____

_____

_____

_____

_____

_____

_____

I understand my wife, by listening to her!

Listening to my wife is a love skill I will utilize to grow my love!

YOUR ABILITY
TO HEAR
MY VOICE
WILL INCREASE
YOUR ABILITY
TO HEAR
YOUR SPOUSE

Enjoy God's goodness today, as He shows you how your wife needs to be loved today.

_____
_____
_____
_____
_____
_____
_____
_____
_____
_____
_____
_____
_____
_____

Use these lines to record God's faithfulness.

_____

_____

_____

_____

_____

_____

_____

_____

_____

_____

_____

_____

_____

_____

_____

_____

_____

Again, I tell you that if two of you on earth agree about anything you ask for, it will be done for you by my Father in heaven. Matthew 18:19

Tools to grow your love

Pray Together

Pray together daily. If you are not feeling the unity, put everything aside and pray together. Your hearts touching God together will always be a healing regimen. Your love will be strengthened as you pray together daily with God.

Paul and Dorthey got married and settled down in a small neighborhood house. They went to the local Brethren church and knew folks in their community, like they were family. This couple farmed their land and Dorthey, was also a School teacher. No matter what was happening, they took time to pray together. Paul and Dorthey had both taught the love of God and they prayed daily together as if it was their last breath. Their children Ken, Keith, Tom and

Ron grew up and had children of their own.

As the years rolled by, Paul and Dorthey's grandchildren grew fast. They loved spending the weekends at their grandparent's house. It was an oasis, away from the world; a place where they went to hear their grandparents touch heaven and seek the face of God. This was a legacy these grandchildren had learned from their parents and grandparents. As they grew, they knew when the storms of life came, God would be there no matter what they were faced with.

Like Paul, you can be a husband who prays with your wife and children regularly. You will find this to be a needed element for the success of your marriage. Praying together will build a bond between you both that cannot be replaced with anything else! You will find miracles taking place, as you both find yourselves surrounded by God's goodness.

Today take the time to think about how you as a husband can incorporate prayer together with your wife. After you meditate on this, fill out the space below. God loves the way you love your wife, and He loves the way you love Him!

We will pray together daily at

_____*o'clock*

We know our prayers will make a difference in our marriage and the lives of those around us!

Your prayers move mountains!

YOUR UNITY *in prayer moves* MY HEART

As you spend time with God today,
write down the things He shares with you
as He shows you how to love your wife.

_____

_____

_____

_____

_____

_____

_____

_____

_____

_____

_____

_____

_____

_____

_____

_____

Use these lines to record God's faithfulness.

_____
_____
_____
_____
_____
_____
_____
_____
_____
_____
_____
_____
_____
_____
_____
_____
_____
_____

Therefore encourage one another and build each other up, just as in fact you are doing.
I Thessalonians 5:11

Tools to grow your love

Cultivate Her Gifts

Look for the gifts and abilities in your wife's hand and help cultivate these gifts. Encourage her to be everything that God has purposed for her to be. **Heaven Is cheering you on, while you stand as, her biggest cheerleader.**

Wyatt and Heather had not known each other exceptionally long before they got married. They fell in love, said their, I do's and enjoyed getting to know their spouse's characteristics, hobbies, and likes. Wyatt and Heather would take long walks at night, talking about the day and their future together. Wyatt wanted children and Heather considered being a mother a gift from God. As they grew closer in conservation, their love grew the more they learned about each other. Wyatt learned his wife had wanted to own her own store. She had a talent of making crafty things. Heather could take things people would normally throw away and make a priceless item out of it. The more Wyatt heard about the things she made, the more he was intrigued.

One day, Wyatt heard about a talent show in their community and he signed his loving wife up for the competition. When Heather came home that night Wyatt told her about the competition and her entry into the contest. The winner would walk away with a grand prize of $5,000.00 dollars. Heather went to the attic and pulled out the things she had made and showed them to Wyatt. He was convinced she would win. Heather got more excited as the date for the contest approached. Wyatt had encouraged his wife with his words and actions. No matter how the contest ended she would always be a winner in his book.

Today, look for opportunities where **you can encourage your wife with her gifts and abilities.** You can be your wife's biggest fan as you encourage her with the many things, she is good at. What are your wife's gifts and abilities? What does she do well?

On the lines below write out the things you see your wife doing well!
My wife's gifts and abilities are,

_____

_____

_____

_____

_____

_____

_____

_____

I know my encouragement can motivate my wife to be all that God has placed within her!

Seizing every opportunity to encourage your wife will make you wise!

YOU WILL DWELL IN

heavenly places and be known as

A MAN AFTER MY HEART

God hovers over you with answers to the questions that lay upon your heart.

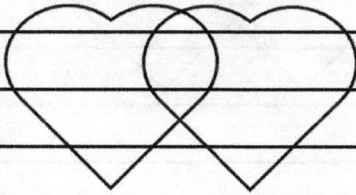

Use these lines to record God's faithfulness.

_____

_____

_____

_____

_____

_____

_____

_____

_____

_____

_____

_____

_____

_____

_____

_____

_____

Come, let us sing for joy to the LORD, let us shout aloud
to the Rock of our salvation.
Psalms 95:1

142

Tools to grow your love

Worship God Together

Take time to sing together, it may be in the car, at home or relaxing on the sofa. Singing together will always put joy in your hearts and grow your love into a deeper place. God loves the way you worship together. He waits daily to hear your praise!

Mark was the worship leader at Kingdom Praise Church. His wife loved to sing together with her husband Mark. One day the two of them were taking a trip to see Brianna's parents. It was a three-hour drive, so the two of them passed the time, by singing and praising God. No matter what was going on in their lives, they always felt closer to God as they spent time together singing and worshiping God. Mark not only sang at church, but at home with his wife. His ability to engage God with his wife grew their love by leaps and bounds.

Today take time to ask God how you can incorporate Him in a greater measure, into your marriage and relationship. God will download ideas to you and show you how to worship together with your wife! He loves you both and His heart is for you!

We will worship at

_____o clock on

_____ Our worship will grow our love!

Worship strengthens our marital bond of unity!

YOU ARE MORE THAN A CONQUEROR YOU ARE A TRANSFORMING AGENT FOR MY KINGDOM

Inhale God's presence today as you feel Him hovering over you. He has all the answers you need!

_____
_____
_____
_____
_____
_____
_____
_____
_____
_____
_____
_____
_____
_____
_____
_____

Use these lines to record God's faithfulness.

_____

_____

_____

_____

_____

_____

_____

_____

_____

_____

_____

_____

_____

_____

_____

_____

_____

And my God will meet all your needs according to His glorious riches in Christ Jesus. Philippians 4:19

Tools to grow your love

Money Matters

Keep your love hats on when discussing money and do not sweat the small stuff. Work together as a team when budgeting and paying bills. Remember to make this a team effort. Acting like you have all the money solutions can stifle your love. Learn from each other grow your love and reinvest your dividends,

Alex was a financial loan officer and he worked for a large firm in his hometown of Smallville. His wife Alice worked as a teller at their local bank. Business was good for them both and together they made a good living.

Although Alice worked at a bank, she was not the financial wizard that Alex was. When Alex needed their financial numbers to put a budget together, he always included Alice in the process. He would take time out to ask for her input to see if the numbers sounded reasonable to her. Although Alex might have known the numbers, his ability to include his wife with her thoughts, grew their love.

As a husband, you will be given multiple opportunities to include your wife and her thoughts in major decisions. Love your wife enough by valuing her thoughts, even if you think you have all the answers. You will find your love growing, as you value her thoughts and input about decisions you both need to make.

Today think about the many ways you could invest your money and secure your future as you value the money you both make.

As a husband, I will plan financially with my wife for a better future!

As I value the money we make, I add value to our marriage!

you will know me
AS JEHOVAH JIREH
your provider

Enjoy God's goodness today, as He shows you how your wife needs to be loved today.

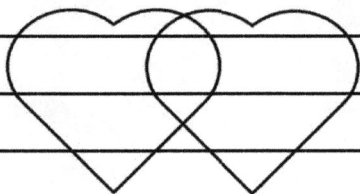

_____

_____

_____

_____

_____

_____

_____

_____

_____

_____

_____

_____

_____

_____

_____

_____

Use these lines to record God's faithfulness.

_____

_____

_____

_____

_____

_____

_____

_____

_____

_____

_____

_____

_____

_____

_____

_____

_____

Do nothing out of selfish ambition or vain conceit, but in humility consider others better than yourselves.
Philippians 2:3

Tools to grow your love

Your Differences

Embrace the differences in each other and accept your wife for who she is. Do not try to control or change her, just enjoy her beauty in the difference she portrays in your marriage. Remember you do not have to think alike, or even agree on the same things. Just agree to disagree and enjoy each other.

Max and Mindy had been married 2 years. They were both more different than you could imagine. Mindy was always cold, and Max was always hot. Mindy ate hot cereal for breakfast and Max ate cold cereal. Mindy was a vegan eater and Max could not eat a meal without meat! The differences between these two were many.

Max began to complain about the heat being on in the summer. Mindy complained about the cupboards being full of cold cereal mix. Max loved Mindy's soft, spoken voice, yet he began to complain about her mumbling and never being able to hear what she was saying.

Without realizing it, they lost the fun in their differences and they began to complain to each other about their differences. Mindy was on the verge of leaving when Max sat down to talk about their differences. He apologized to Mindy for complaining about their differences. He reminded her that he loved her voice, and he was sorry for complaining about not being able to hear her. This young couple worked out their differences and spent time reminding one another of the things they really loved about each other.

As a husband, you will receive many opportunities to complain about your differences or find the fun in your uniqueness. Your efforts in not getting caught up in the many ways in which you are opposite will have huge rewards. Always be willing to accept your wife for who she is, what she enjoys and the things she likes. Your acceptance of your differences will grow your love! On the lines below record your many differences and the fun you can find in your uniqueness.

My differences with my wife are

_____

_____

_____

_____

I can find the fun in our differences by

_____

_____

_____

_____

**Embracing the differences in
each other can be fun!**

*Accepting the differences in
your wife will grow your love
and strengthen your marital
unity!*

MY LIGHT IS SEEN
in and through
YOU

*As you spend time with God today,
write down the things He shares with you
as He shows you how to love your wife.*

Use these lines to record God's faithfulness.

_____

_____

_____

_____

_____

_____

_____

_____

_____

_____

_____

_____

_____

_____

_____

The law of the LORD is perfect, reviving the soul. The statutes of the LORD are trustworthy, making wise the simple. Psalm 19:7

Tools to grow your love

Do a Getaway

Make time for a getaway weekend. You will find your getaway refreshing your soul and recharging your love. Unplugging from the drum and everyday buzz around you will leave you both recharged. Take time to caress your wife's heart with love words.

Mick and Mandy had been married 2 years. They loved each other and enjoyed spending time together at the lake. Mick and Mandy discussed their getaways even before they were married. They knew it would be a need for both to stay focused at work and not get burned out at home. Every two weeks, both of them would pack their bags and head for the lake to spend the weekend on the water. This was a time they could relax together, unwind, and listen to the events of each other's week. Mandy enjoyed every weekend they took off together and Mick knew how important it was for Mandy to regroup. She was an RN at their local General Hospital. It was important for Mandy to regroup after her long work weeks. Mick worked as a lawyer at a large firm and it was also significant for him to unwind on the lake.

Together this amazing couple worked to make sure both had time away from work and home to get refreshed and rejuvenated. Mandy was grateful to Mick for allowing them the time away from home to refresh their minds and souls. Mick considered his wife's need to get away.

Today think about a time you could plan a getaway for you and your wife. Think about a place she would enjoy and make this a time of enjoyment as you both get refreshed and rejuvenated.

Our getaway will be on

_____

_____

_____

We will go to

_____

_____

_____

I love and honor my wife with getaway time!

> Your ability to meet your wife's love needs is a homerun!

you will
REST IN THE
goodness of my
LOVE

God hovers over you with answers to the questions that lay upon your heart.

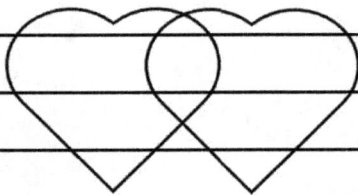

_____

_____

_____

_____

_____

_____

_____

_____

_____

_____

_____

_____

_____

_____

_____

_____

_____

Use these lines to record God's faithfulness.

_____

_____

_____

_____

_____

_____

_____

_____

_____

_____

_____

_____

_____

_____

_____

_____

Be joyful in hope, patient in affliction, faithful in prayer.
Romans 12:12

Tools to grow your Love

Your Actions

Your actions will always speak louder than your words so be careful of the things you do. If you want to caress the heart of your wife and grow your love, keep your actions full of love! This is a priceless tool to practice daily.

Seth and Sarah were in love. They had dated 1 ½ years before they got married and they both knew how to make each other feel loved and valued. Seth would daily thank Sarah for the lunch she fixed him, and Sarah would remind Seth that he completed her. The love actions between this couple; blessed their friends and their co-workers.

They were in love and they were not afraid to let the whole world know. Their love grew with every love action. No matter what was happening, this love couple chose to give each other grace daily. They utilized the tool of forgiveness and valued each other with every moment they shared together. Seth used every opportunity to love his wife and value her. His love acts to Sarah motivated her to love him better.

As a husband, everyday will be an opportunity to show your wife love actions. Do not assume she knows how you feel. Be intentional and love her on purpose! Fill out the lines below and grow your love!

I will show my wife love actions by

_____

_____

_____

_____

_____

_____

_____

I will increase my love actions by

_____
_____
_____
_____
_____
_____
_____
_____
_____
_____

**I honor my wife with
love actions!**

*Loving my wife is a
decision I choose to make
daily!*

YOUR LIFE IS
MARKED BY MY HAND

Inhale God's presence today as you feel Him hovering over you. He has all the answers you need!

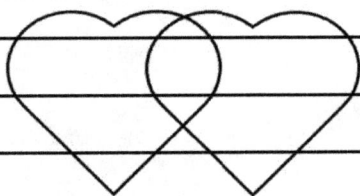

_____
_____
_____
_____
_____
_____
_____
_____
_____
_____
_____
_____
_____
_____
_____
_____
_____

Use these lines to record God's faithfulness.

_____

_____

_____

_____

_____

_____

_____

_____

_____

_____

_____

_____

_____

_____

_____

_____

Marriage should be honored by all, and the marriage bed kept pure, for God will judge the adulterer and all the sexually immoral. Hebrews 13:4

Tools to grow your love

Stay Committed

Keep your eyes and admiration for your wife only. Remember to view her as a precious, priceless, gift from God. Your value in her will increase your value in your marriage. Value commitment, as you esteem your wife with the highest regards. Heaven rejoices over your purity.

Greg and Laura had been married six months when Laura packed her bags and decided to move back home. Greg tried to convince her that he loved her, but the pornography magazines Laura found hiding in his drawer, told her something else. Greg knew he had issues with pornography. He

172

tried to quit, but he kept feeling a pull from time to time to buy magazines. When Laura moved back home, Greg showered her with love letters, texts, and phone calls.

Greg asked her one day if she would consider going to marriage counseling with their minister. Laura agreed and they met with their Pastor that Sunday after the service. Greg opened his heart and began to share with Pastor Smith some of his issues and how it had driven Laura away. Pastor Smith prayed with them both and asked them to come in for counseling on a weekly basis so he could help them resolve their issues. With the help of God, praying together and counseling with their pastor, they were able to work through their issues. Greg became a faithful husband with eyes and a heart for only Laura.

It is important as a husband to have eyes for only your wife. As you pray together you will find God building the bond between you both. Greg could have blamed his wife, but he did not. He took responsibility for his actions and made every effort to become a strong leader for righteousness in his marriage and home.

Today ask God to increase the purity in your heart and help you live with eyes for only your wife. Your role as a husband is important to God. He will help you lead with a righteous heart!

I will stay committed to my wife by

_____

_____

_____

_____

_____

_____

_____

To protect my eyes and heart, I will refrain from

_____

_____

_____

_____

_____

_____

_____

_____

_____

_____

Commitment is a priceless tool that will grow my love for my wife!

Commitment is a key for marital success!

YOU ARE A REFLECTION OF MY HEART AND GOODNESS TO OTHERS

Enjoy God's goodness today, as He shows you how your wife needs to be loved today.

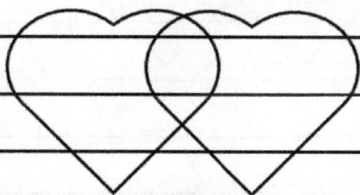

_____

_____

_____

_____

_____

_____

_____

_____

_____

_____

_____

_____

_____

_____

_____

Use these lines to record God's faithfulness.

_____

_____

_____

_____

_____

_____

_____

_____

_____

_____

_____

_____

_____

_____

_____

_____

_____

_____

You will be a crown of splendor in the LORD'S hand, a royal diadem in the hand of your God. Isaiah 62:3

Tools to grow your love

Value Your Wife

Look for opportunities to show your wife value. Viewing her as priceless gold will cultivate appreciation in your relationship. She will feel treasured and your love will grow immensely. Remember your actions are seeds. Continue to plant good seeds daily.

William and Betty had not been married exceedingly long. Their love for each other grew with the days on the calendar. William had been married before and his wife of six years had passed away from cancer. William had learned to value life with every moment that came. When he married Betty, he knew not to take anything for granted. He valued his wife with his responses, tone in his voice, and with his actions.

179

Betty felt valued, honored, and respected in their marriage and relationship. Betty likewise reciprocated this same value back to William. She was grateful to find a man who loved her in word and action. She found ways daily to thank William for valuing her as his wife. This amazing husband left an impact on his wife as he continually honored her.

No matter what kind of marriage you are having, it is key to treasure your wife with honor and respect. She will feel your love and notice the way you value your marriage. As a husband, you will receive multiple opportunities daily, to value your wife.

Today think about the many ways you value your wife and how you can show your wife more value.

I value my wife by

_____

_____

_____

_____

I can increase my value for my wife by

_____

_____

_____

_____

_____

_____

_____

_____

_____

I love my wife by valuing her!

My wife is a gift from God I value and treasure!

I ENJOY
the beauty
YOU
radiate as
YOU HONOR
each other

As you spend time with God today,
write down the things He shares with you
as He shows you how to love your wife.

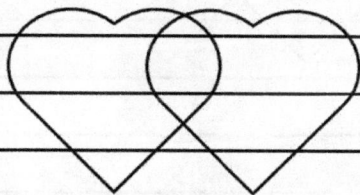

_____

_____

_____

_____

_____

_____

_____

_____

_____

_____

_____

_____

_____

_____

_____

Use these lines to record God's faithfulness.

_____

_____

_____

_____

_____

_____

_____

_____

_____

_____

_____

_____

_____

_____

_____

_____

_____

_____

He who walks with the wise grows wise, but a
companion of fools suffers harm. Proverbs 13:20

184

Tools to grow your love

Cultivate Friendships

Cultivate friendships with other married couples. Being married and hanging with only single friends apart from your wife can deplete your love. Ask God to bring Godly married friends into your life. Your love skills are growing!

Nick got married to his best friend Angela. They became husband and wife and remain best friends. No matter what was happening Nick knew he could talk to Angela about anything. Six months later, Nick started having issues with his friends from work. They were single and wanted to hang with Nick 3 and 4 times a week. When he turned down their offer to hang, he would get the cold shoulder and an attitude from them the next day at work. Nick told Angela he needed to find some new friends to hang with.

Angela listened to the heart of her husband and then suggested they attend a marriage group at church. They went on Wednesday night and met some young married couples. Nick and Angela found themselves encouraged as they became better acquainted with other Christian couples. Nick put his relationship with Angela above his co-workers. His actions echoed the amount of love he had for his wife.

As a Godly husband, hanging with good married couples will help nourish your relationship and grow your love. Take time today to think about the relationships you have and if they are good friendships to keep.

My friendships should

_____

_____

_____

_____

_____

_____

_____

_____

_____

_____

_____

_____

_____

_____

_____

_____

_____

_____

_____

My toxic friendships I will end to grow my love with my wife and nourish my marriage!

> *I can create a marriage with friendship on fire!*

FOR I HAVE PLACED AN

OVERCOMING SPIRIT

WITHIN YOU AND YOU WILL

RISE ABOVE EVEN THE NEGATIVE

God hovers over you with answers to the questions that lay upon your heart.

_____

_____

_____

_____

_____

_____

_____

_____

_____

_____

_____

_____

_____

_____

_____

_____

_____

Use these lines to record God's faithfulness.

_____

_____

_____

_____

_____

_____

_____

_____

_____

_____

_____

_____

_____

_____

Trust in the Lord with all your heart and lean not on your own understanding; and in all your ways acknowledge Him, and He will make your paths straight.
Proverbs 3:5-6

190

Tools to grow your love

Grow Your Trust

Focus on growing your trust in your wife along with your trust in God. Think good things about your wife; give her positive regard and always trust. You will find your trust for your wife growing as you deepen your trust in God. Your Love skills are amazing!

Edward and Edna had been married for 5 years. They loved each other but, they both had struggled in their relationship at times. Edward had been married before to a woman who could not be faithful. Edna was also married to a man who had left her for a woman 15 years younger than her. This couple had carried baggage from previous relationships into their marriage. Although they were both wanting to make it work, they were struggling with the chaos their hearts were carrying.

One night, Edward asked Edna if she would consider going to church with him. She quickly agreed and said, "That would be great!" They went to their local church that Sunday and decided together to put God in the center of their marriage.

That night before they went to bed, they prayed together asking God to forgive them for not loving each other better. Edward knew no matter what their relationship felt like, God, had the answer they needed. As they both opened their hearts to God, He healed their hearts and increased their trust for each other.

No matter what situation you are faced with, God has the answer. He will help you love your wife and be the Godly husband you need to be.

Father God,

I am needing you to help me trust my wife. I am asking you to help me be the Godly husband you have called me to be. I ask you to give me the strength I need in every situation and circumstance. I am asking for your help. I love you God.

Amen

Your trust makes a difference!

On the lines below, list the many ways you can trust your wife in a greater way.

_____

_____

_____

_____

_____

_____

_____

_____

Your love skills are amazing!
Keep growing your trust!

your trust in

ME INCREASES

your trust in your wife

30 Day Recap

_____

_____

_____

_____

_____

_____

_____

_____

_____

_____

_____

_____

_____

_____

_____

_____

YOU ARE

The joy

OF MY HEART

you are a man after
MY HEART AND I WILL
write my precepts upon the walls of
YOUR HEART AND YOU
will walk in my ways
AND MY RIGHTEOUSNESS WILL GUIDE YOU,
as you love your wife
WITH MY LOVE, YOU WILL
be an example to many
OF MY GOODNESS AND FOREVER FAITHFULNESS

www.ingramcontent.com/pod-product-compliance
Lightning Source LLC
Chambersburg PA
CBHW060825050426
42453CB00008B/586